FATHERS AND SONS

NOTES

including
Life and Background
A Note on Russian Names
List of Characters
General Plot Summary
Chapter Summaries and Commentaries
Character Analyses
Structure of Fathers and Sons
Review Questions
Selected Bibliography

by
Denis M. Calandra, M.A.
University of Nebraska
and
James L. Roberts, Ph.D.
Department of English
University of Nebraska

D0104259

Cliffs Notes

INCORPORATED

LINCOLN, NEBRASKA   68501

ISBN 0-8220-0470-4

©Copyright 1966
by
C. K. Hillegass
All Rights Reserved
Printed in U.S.A.

CONTENTS

LIFE AND BACKGROUND 5

A NOTE ON RUSSIAN NAMES 6

LIST OF CHARACTERS 7

GENERAL PLOT SUMMARY 8

CHAPTER SUMMARIES AND COMMENTARIES

    Chapter 1 10

    Chapters 2, 3 12

    Chapter 4 14

    Chapter 5 16

    Chapters 6, 7 19

    Chapters 8, 9 22

    Chapter 10 25

    Chapter 11 28

    Chapters 12, 13 30

    Chapter 14 31

    Chapter 15 33

    Chapter 16 34

    Chapter 17 37

    Chapter 18 40

    Chapter 19 41

    Chapter 20 43

    Chapter 21 44

    Chapter 22 47

    Chapter 23 48

    Chapter 24 49

    Chapter 25 53

    Chapter 26 54

    Chapter 27 56

    Chapter 28 58

CHARACTER ANALYSES 59

STRUCTURE OF "FATHERS AND SONS" 63

REVIEW QUESTIONS 65

SELECTED BIBLIOGRAPHY 66

FATHERS AND SONS

LIFE AND BACKGROUND

Ivan Sergeyevitch Turgenev was born of wealthy parents in the city of Oryol, central Russia, on October 28, 1818. He spent most of his childhood on the family estate under the instruction of tutors until he enrolled at the University of Moscow in 1833. Before a year had passed he transferred to the University of Petersburg, from which he graduated in 1837.

Turgenev traveled for some time in Europe, especially Germany, and chiefly studied philosophy. In 1843, he accepted a minor post in the Ministry of the Interior and also made the acquaintance of Pauline Viardot, a sophisticated French singer whom he would remain devoted to for the rest of his life and for whose sake he would often remain abroad for long periods of time.

After retiring from the service, he went to France, spending summers on the Viardot's estate and winters in Paris. This French period proved to be a very fertile one in his literary career, for it was here that he wrote most of the pieces which later (August, 1852) were to comprise his *A Sportsman's Sketches*. Turgenev had witnessed the February Revolution in Paris (1848) and his subsequent connection with reform groups in Russia and his eulogy of the recently deceased but highly "suspect" Gogol in 1852 led to his arrest and one-month imprisonment in Petersburg.

By the mid-1850's, he was spending as much time in Europe as in Russia, and in 1857 Pauline Viardot gave birth to a child allegedly Turgenev's. In August of 1860 on the Isle of Wight, he conceived the idea for his *Fathers and Sons;* he finished the novel in July of 1861 in Russia.

In 1863, he was summoned to answer charges of having aided a London group of expatriates, but was soon exonerated, bought land at Baden near the Viardots and settled there. In 1869, he ran into financial difficulties and had to sell his newly built villa, but remained there as a tenant while he prepared an edition of his collected works. Some of those finished to date were *Rudin* (1855), *A Nest of Gentlefolk* (1859), *On the Eve* (1860), and *Smoke* (1867), and several dramas.

During the next ten years, Turgenev worked on his novel, *Virgin Soil,* and several more plays, spending time in Baden, Paris, Great Britain, and Russia. In 1879, his brother Nikolai died, and upon Turgenev's arrival in Moscow, he was celebrated by the liberals. This same year he received an honorary degree from Oxford and began to prepare another collection of his works. Always a great admirer of Pushkin, he took an active part in the Pushkin festival of 1880. In 1882, he was taken seriously ill, but continued to work, dictating "Fire at the Sea" and "The End." He died in France on September 3, 1883, with Madame Viardot and her children about him. The year before his death, he published a sheaf of what he called "an old man's jottings" under the title of *Poems in Prose.*

A NOTE ON RUSSIAN NAMES

The middle names of all male characters end in "-vitch" and of all female characters in "-ovna." This ending simply means the "son of" or "daughter of" the father whose first name is converted into their middle name. For example, Nikolai's father was named "Petro." Thus, both Pavel and Nikolai have the name "Petrovitch" for their middle name. This middle name is called the *Patronymic.* All Russians have three names and might be called by any one or any combination of these names.

The spelling of the Russian name might differ slightly from one translation to another because a transliteration must be made, and since English cannot reproduce absolutely exactly certain Russian graphemes, an approximation must suffice. In pronouncing these names, if the reader will remember to give the vowels their "continental" value and pronounce the consonants as in English, a rough approximation to the Russian pronunciation will be obtained. The consonant "kh" sounds rather like the Scottish "ch" in "loch"; the "zh" represents a sound like "s" in "measure"; and the final "v" is pronounced "f".

LIST OF CHARACTERS

Nikolai Petrovitch Kirsanov
A small landowner in a rural part of Russia who has attempted to keep up with modern ideas.

Arkady Nikolayevitch Kirsanov
His son, who has been studying in St. Petersburg and who has come under the influence of a new philosophy called nihilism.

Pavel Petrovitch Kirsanov
Nikolai's brother, who believes strongly in preserving the aristocratic mode of life.

Fenichka
Nikolai's housekeeper, the mother of his young son, and eventually his wife. She is almost always referred to by her nickname, Fenichka. Her real name is Fedosya Nikolayevna Savishna.

Mitya
Nikolai and Fenichka's young son.

Yevgeny Vassilievitch Bazarov
A friend of Arkady's who professes a philosophy of nihilism.

Viktor Sitnikov
An acquaintance of Bazarov's who tries to attach himself to popular causes.

Avdotya Nikitishna Kukshina
A friend of Sitnikov's who professes to be a liberated woman.

Anna Sergeyevna Odintsova
A wealthy widow who is reputed to be quite advanced and liberal.

Katerine Sergeyevna Lokteva (Katya)
Madame Odintsova's sister, who attracts the attention of Arkady, and is eventually married to him.

Vassily Ivanovitch Bazarov
Bazarov's devoted father, who is a retired army doctor and who has tried to keep up with the latest advancements in medicine.

Arina Vlassevna Bazarov
Bazarov's mother; the traditional conglomeration of sentiment, superstition, and doting love for her offspring.

Princess Abdotya Stepanovna
Madame Odintsova's old and aristocratic aunt.

Matvei Ilyich Kolyazin
The "uncle" whom Arkady visits in a neighboring province.

Porfiry Platonovitch
Madame Odintsova's neighbor who often comes for conversation and cards.

Father Aleksei
The priest in Bazarov's home town.

Prokofitch
A servant at Marino who adheres to the old principles of the Russian aristocracy.

Piotr
Another servant at Marino; emancipated and "modern."

Dunyasha
A servant at Marino who is fond of Bazarov.

Timofeich and *Anfisushka*
Two of Vassily Ivanovitch Bazarov's servants.

GENERAL PLOT SUMMARY

Arkady Kirsanov has just graduated from the University of Petersburg and returns with a friend, Bazarov, to his father's modest estate in an outlying province of Russia. The father gladly receives the two young men at his estate, called Marino, but Nikolai's brother, Pavel, soon becomes upset by the strange new philosophy called "nihilism" which the young men advocate.

Nikolai feels awkward with his son at home, partially because Arkady's views have dated his own beliefs, and partially because he has taken a servant, Fenichka, into his house to live with him and has already had a son by her.

The two young men remain at Marino for a short time, then decide to visit a relative of Arkady's in a neighboring province. There they observe the local gentry and meet Madame Odintsova, an elegant woman of independent means who invites them to spend a few days at her estate, Nikolskoe.

At Nikolskoe, they also meet Katya, Madame Odintsova's sister, who attracts Arkady. They remain for a short period and Bazarov is more and more drawn toward Madame Odintsova, until he finally announces that he loves her. She does not respond to his declaration, and soon after, Arkady and Bazarov leave for Bazarov's home.

At Bazarov's home, they are received enthusiastically by his parents. Bazarov is still disturbed by his rejection, and is difficult to get along with. He almost comes to blows with his friend Arkady. After a brief stay, they decide to return to Marino, and circle by to see Madame Odintsova, who receives them coolly. They leave almost immediately and return to Arkady's home.

Arkady remains for only a few days, and makes an excuse to leave in order to see Katya. Bazarov stays at Marino to do some scientific research, and tension between him and Pavel increases. Bazarov enjoys talking with Fenichka and playing with her child, and one day he gives her a quick, harmless kiss which is observed by Pavel. The older man feels it is his duty to defend his brother's honor, and he challenges Bazarov to a duel. Pavel is wounded slightly, and Bazarov must leave Marino. He stops for an hour or so at Madame Odintsova's, then continues on to his parents' home. Meanwhile, Arkady and Katya have fallen in love and have become engaged.

At home, Bazarov cannot keep his mind on his work and while performing an autopsy fails to take the proper precautions. He contracts typhus, and on his deathbed, sends for Madame Odintsova, who arrives in time to hear Bazarov tell her how beautiful she is.

Arkady marries Katya and takes over the management of his father's estate. His father marries Fenichka and is delighted to have his son home with him. Pavel leaves the country and lives the rest of his life as a "noble" in Dresden, Germany.

SUMMARIES AND COMMENTARIES

CHAPTER 1

Summary

Nikolai Petrovitch Kirsanov and his servant Piotr are waiting the arrival of Arkady, Nikolai's son, who has recently finished his studies at the University of St. Petersburg and is returning to his country home for a visit. Nikolai is a landlord with a moderate estate. He is the son of a Russian general who had achieved a degree of fame in the front lines of 1812. Unlike his brother Pavel, who excelled in military service, Nikolai "could never distinguish himself by his courage." Later the two brothers shared an apartment in St. Petersburg, where Nikolai finished his studies at the university.

Nikolai married the daughter of his landlord in spite of the objections of his father, and settled in the country, where Arkady was born. His wife died prematurely, leaving Nikolai lonely and isolated. When Arkady came of age, his father went with him to St. Petersburg and remained there with him for three school years while Arkady pursued his studies. The final winter, Nikolai was unable to remain with Arkady and is now nostalgically recalling the past while waiting for the arrival of his son. During his daydreaming, the coach carrying Arkady arrives and the father and son lock in an embrace.

Commentary

Turgenev was a writer intently interested in social reforms, and as a realistic novelist, he set his works in contemporary Russia. Thus, the background and the social changes going on in Russia at the time do function in his novel. Ultimately, Bazarov must be seen as one of the rising new middle class which will dominate the scene in Russia for the next generations. Previous to the 1840's and 1850's, the middle class was virtually nonexistent as a social power, but during these decades, this class began to produce its own intelligentsia which asserted itself in many areas of Russian life. The contrast between a member of the old school such as Pavel with Bazarov, the new middle class, will be developed at length later in the novel.

The relationship between the great landowner and the serf was undergoing a tremendous change also. The situation in Russia during this time is analogous to the conditions found in the southern states of America in the 1840's and the 1850's. The serfs were actually similar to the black slaves in that they lived completely at the mercy of the wealthy landowner. In 1862, the serfs were granted complete freedom, but before that time, most of the more advanced landowners and thinkers had voluntarily freed their serfs in the manner that Kirsanov and Bazarov had done. Earlier, a person's wealth was often evaluated in terms of the number of serfs he owned, and thus we have the expression that the estate was valued at two hundred "souls." By the time of this novel, the word "souls" was used satirically as "baptized property." Turgenev is aware of the basic contradiction involved in recognizing the serfs as Christian souls and some landowner's personal property at the same time.

Thus the first chapter gives us an indication that this was a time of change. Turgenev refers to Piotr as one of the "new, emancipated servants."

Early in the first chapter, we are introduced to a technique that Turgenev employs often. In this case, he interrupts the narrative briefly and addresses the reader directly in order to give us some background information. Later realists will not enter so directly into the narrative. Turgenev uses both the traditional nineteenth-century technique of speaking directly to the reader and the more recent technique of presenting scenes directly without author intrusion.

In the background information, we discover that Nikolai has spent a great deal of time in St. Petersburg while Arkady was enrolled in school there and has in the past had a close relationship with his son. This must be kept in mind when we observe the tension that will soon develop between the father and son. We are also made aware of a certain romantic bent in Nikolai's nature as we observe him dreaming of his past happiness. As soon as Arkady appears, Nikolai will rapidly learn to conceal his romantic thoughts.

Keeping in mind the title of the novel, we realize then the importance of Turgenev's building and expressing directly the exact nature of the father's personality so that he will be seen in contrast to his son's newer and more advanced ways of thinking.

CHAPTERS 2, 3

Summary

Arkady has brought a friend from the university with him whom he introduces as Bazarov. Nikolai is pleased to receive any friend of his son and asks to be informed of his "christian name and patronymic," which is Yevgeny Vassilievitch. Bazarov is tall and thin with a peaceful smile which suggests a degree of self-confidence. He holds himself aloof and does not strike one as being overly friendly on first glance.

Arkady and his father get in the buggy while Bazarov must ride in another conveyance and they depart for the farm. On the way home, Arkady is filled with joy at being reunited with his father again, but he keeps the conversation on a prosaic level so as to discourage his father from becoming over-emotional. Thus, they discuss only the more mundane subjects and Arkady tells Nikolai how important his friendship with Bazarov is. Arkady is convinced that Bazarov is an intellectual giant and wants great care taken of him.

As they drive home, they discuss the problems which Nikolai has encountered during the year that they have been separated. Nikolai has been changing his farm system, trying to remove the serfs and establish them as tenant farmers (or a type of share cropper.)

Nikolai is very sentimental about the farm and the place where his son was born, but Arkady cuts him by saying that it makes no difference where a man is born, indicating an anti-romantic view. Nikolai is somewhat astonished by his son's statement and does not immediately recover.

Nikolai tries to warn his son that one of the servants is now living in the house—the young Fenichka—and tries to apologize for living with this person of "inferior rank." Nikolai expects his son to be shocked, and is surprised when Arkady expresses himself so liberally as to give the impression of not caring in the least that his father has taken a mistress. Nikolai wonders if this fact won't embarrass their guest, Bazarov, but Arkady assures him that Bazarov is a person not to be anxious about.

As they reach the farm, Arkady notices that the place has fallen into a state of degeneration. Soon they arrive at the farmhouse, which Nikolai calls "Marino."

Commentary

The extent of devotion between Nikolai and Arkady is seen in their greetings. There is no tension between them at the present moment and later we will observe that the tension that does develop will be caused largely by Bazarov.

To understand the meaning of Nikolai's question "May I know your Christian name and patronymic?" see the section on the meaning of Russian names.

Note again that Piotr follows his role of the emancipated servant because he refuses to kiss his master's hand in the fashion of the older servants and only bows to Arkady.

At the beginning of the novel and the ride to the estate, Bazarov is separated from Arkady and Nikolai, and must ride in a separate vehicle. Thus at the beginning, Nikolai and his son are together while Bazarov is the outsider. But gradually through the next chapters, we will see a growing separation between Nikolai and Arkady and a closer connection between the two young people. Ultimately, however, Arkady and his father will emerge as the true companions.

On the ride back to the farm, we see the portending separation between father and son. For example, Nikolai thinks that Arkady should be very excited to be returning to his old birthplace, but Arkady cuts his father by saying that it makes no difference where a man is born. After this interchange, there is silence for a long part of the journey. The technique of this small scene is also important. It is presented objectively and dramatically with no author comment or intrusion.

Nikolai brings up the important subject of Fenichka. Arkady's reaction is important because his father is over-apologetic about this somewhat unorthodox relationship, but Arkady feels that he has advanced beyond such insignificant moral discriminations and is filled "with a half-secretive feeling of superiority towards his good, softhearted father."

Turgenev continues to build this contrast between the two generations as Nikolai, the father, looks at the landscape and begins to quote from a Pushkin poem. Pushkin was the father of Russian romanticism and is later the butt of ridicule by Bazarov. Thus, Nikolai is grounded not only in romantic poetry but in the cultural past of Russia, while the young people want to discard all the past.

CHAPTER 4

Summary

Upon arrival at Marino, they are met by Prokofitch, who is described as a simpering old servant. He fawns over the young son of the master and conducts himself in an obeisant manner. Nikolai orders a meal to be prepared immediately and Arkady wants to clean up, but before he leaves, his uncle Pavel appears. He shakes hands with Arkady in a European fashion and then embraces his nephew three times in the Russian fashion.

After Arkady and Bazarov leave to go to their rooms, Pavel asks about the "hairy" creature who is visiting with Arkady.

Bazarov immediately begins to mock Pavel as soon as they are parted. He finds Pavel to be terribly affected for some one living so far out in the country, and in contrast, he finds Nikolai to be very likable. During dinner, Arkady pours himself an extra glass of wine and drinks much more than he usually does.

After returning to their room that night, Bazarov comments about Pavel's affectations and his unique European demeanor. In Pavel's room, long after others have gone to bed, Pavel stays up dressed quite properly and stares about the room. In another room, Fenichka is also awake, but she keeps herself out of sight. In a motherly fashion, she constantly looks in upon her child.

Commentary

Chapter 4 presents the arrival home, but Turgenev lets us know that the event is different from what it would have been in the past. Before the new ideas came into prominence, all the servants would have been gathered around to greet the arrival of the young master, but now this form of activity is frowned upon as being archaic. We do see that Fenichka peeks out of the window and then disappears. More important is the contrast between the two types of servants represented by Piotr and Prokofitch. As noted earlier, Piotr is the new liberated type of servant, but Prokofitch belongs to the old school. Therefore, the latter comes forward and kisses his young master's hand.

We meet Arkady's uncle for the first time. He will stand in contrast to everything that Bazarov represents. Pavel consciously affects European habits of dress and actions. He is an elegant and aristocratic man, immediately repulsed by Bazarov's appearance. Pavel delights in throwing out French phrases and makes every effort to appear Europeanized. One should be aware that during a certain period of Russian history, the educated Russian did correspond mainly in French and used Russian only in communication with the serfs or other low-class servants. In fact many Russians could not read and write the Russian language and knew only the necessary minimum to be able to communicate with the serfs.

We notice for the first time that Arkady is uneasy over his return home. He has outgrown childhood, but now returning to the scene of his past, it is difficult to assume his new role. Arkady is drawn between two loyalties: one to his home and his background and the other to his new friend with the advanced ideas. Arkady tries to defend his uncle, whom he respects in many ways and dislikes the fact that Bazarov refers to him as an "archaic phenomenon."

As much as Arkady tries to deny it objectively, we see that he and his father are essentially alike. He acknowledges that his father is a timid man, but the reader also knows that Arkady is himself rather timid.

The chapter ends on Fenichka as she looks at her sleeping baby. Without knowing it at present, we are being prepared for the fact that the child is actually Arkady's half brother even though his father is not married.

CHAPTER 5

Summary

The next morning, Bazarov arises before anyone else and goes out to catch some frogs for scientific experiments. He notices the broken down condition of the land, and talks freely with a couple of the peasants. Meanwhile, at the house, Nikolai feels compelled to explain in more detail his association with Fenichka. He tells Arkady about their peculiar relationship, and Arkady responds with an air of indifference saying: "Well, you know my philosophy of life, and I would hardly want to interfere with your life or your happiness." Arkady felt that "he was being magnanimous."

Arkady leaves his father abruptly in order to go and greet Fenichka and discovers that she has a child. In a joking sort of manner, he berates his father for not having told him about his new brother.

Pavel then asks Arkady about his friend Bazarov, and hears that he is a nihilist. Both Nikolai and Pavel are astonished by this term and try to figure out what it means. They know that it comes from the Latin word *nihil,* which means "nothing." Upon further discussion, Pavel maintains that a "nihilist" must be one who respects nothing.

Shortly after this, Fenichka arrives to serve cocoa, and we see that she is a rather pretty person who is uneasy in the presence of others. Soon, Bazarov returns from the swamps, all bespotted with mud from his excursion after frogs. He is greeted sarcastically by Pavel as "Mr. Nihilist."

Commentary

The beginning of the chapter informs us about Bazarov's character. He is a scientist and a rationalist who believes that the workings of human beings aren't much different from the workings of a frog. He approaches everything with as much scientific objectivity as possible and will ultimately maintain that human feelings and concepts should be viewed either as nonsense or as only so much weakness in the human body.

The conflict between Arkady and Nikolai increases when Nikolai tries to explain his relationship with Fenichka, and Arkady assumes the role of the more advanced person who could not be disturbed by any form of unorthodox social relationship. Nikolai does not know how to accept these foreign ideas and is thrown into confusion by them. We should note here that Russia of the nineteenth century was strictly divided into definite social classes. Fenichka was a member of the lower class who would not be accepted by the wealthy class to which Nikolai belonged. In the true sense of the word, he married a *servant,* who is socially inferior to him. The point is that the old aristocratic order is so firmly embedded in Nikolai's mind that he can't really justify his relationship with Fenichka as proper, and thus he is thrown into confusion when his son so calmly accepts the fact. We should also be aware that when Arkady is being so magnanimous, he is consiciously aware that he is doing so.

We first hear the word *nihilist* in this chapter. Even though this word is common now, it was first coined by Turgenev to describe the type of person represented by Bazarov. When the subject first comes up, Bazarov is not present and the meaning of the term is explained by Arkady. A nihilist is a person who "examines everything from a critical point of view....a person who does not bow to any authorities; who doesn't accept any principle on faith, no matter how hallowed and how venerated the principle is." In contrast, Pavel is proud and arrogant that he is one of the representatives of the old century. He believes that without principles it is impossible to exist.

With the presentation of these ideas, Turgenev introduces one of his main themes, which is the conflict between the romantic past and the realistic present. Pavel stands for the old traditional and romantic past and he can never break away from this past to become a functional man of the present world. He insists on maintaining old views, even though he never bothers to examine the underlying truths of these beliefs. In contrast, Bazarov will reject all things of the past without examining to see if they might possess some values. In their own ways, both of them are mistaken.

Fenichka appears for the first time. She feels insecure because she is not officially married and is furthermore conscious of her inferior social position. Likewise, she is aware that Nikolai has not accepted her as an equal; thus she makes a point of remaining in the background.

Two small details humorously indicate the difference between Pavel and Bazarov. Bazarov notes that Pavel insists on using fancy English washbasins, while at the same time the doors to the house don't work. Pavel notes that Bazarov "doesn't believe in principles, but he believes in frogs."

Summary

Bazarov joins the others at tea, and Pavel begins interrogating Bazarov about his beliefs. Pavel makes derisive comments about Bazarov's admiration for the German scientists. Bazarov tells Pavel that he doesn't "believe" in anything, whether it be science, art or human institutions, but he does pay special attention to science because it "gives him the facts."

Pavel and Nikolai leave to go talk with the overseer, and both are upset over what they have heard from the young people. They can't understand why youth has rejected so much that the old people hold valuable. They are both perplexed, but of the two Pavel is angrier.

When the two of them are alone, Bazarov asks his friend Arkady if Pavel always acts the way he just has. He makes several derogatory comments about Pavel. Arkady defends him, maintaining that Pavel's life story demands some sympathy; then he proceeds to tell Pavel's life story.

Pavel was, in his youth, a "remarkably handsome" person who made women lose "their wits over him," and provoked men to call him a fop. He won fame for his daring feats and dexterity in athletics. Even though every woman in the country was at his feet, he once met an enigmatic noble lady who could never give herself to him entirely. She was not a particularly witty person nor exceptionally beautiful, but she did possess a bizarre and haunting appeal. Pavel was entranced by her, and after a prolonged affair, the mysterious lady grew tired of him. After she left him, he followed her through most of Europe, and for a short time they resumed their relationship. But when they separated this time, it was for good. For some time, Pavel mourned his loss. He resigned his position in the army and finally retired to his brother's farm, where he has lived ever since.

Thus, Arkady feels that one must judge Pavel with special consideration because his life has been so frustrated. Besides that,

Pavel had been most generous in helping Nikolai financially whenever the need arose. Bazarov, rather than being sympathetic, is quite sarcastic and maintains that any person who allows himself to stake his life "on the card of women's love" is not a man but simply a "male animal." Arkady tries to explain that Pavel grew up in a different time, but Bazarov cynically maintains that "It's all romanticism, nonsense, rottenness, art." He prefers to go and look at some frogs or beetles.

Commentary

The reader should be highly aware of the visual images presented in the first part of chapter 6. The intent is to continue the development of the antagonism between Pavel and Bazarov. The visual image is that of Bazarov, who has just returned from collecting frogs in the marshes, extremely dirty and soiled as contrasted with the immaculately clean and precisely dressed Pavel. The sight of the filthy Bazarov entering the house is basically repulsive to the fastidious Pavel, whose "aristocratic nature was revolted by Bazarov's completely free and easy manner."

The argument between Pavel and Bazarov is a result of their basic views. Pavel dislikes Bazarov's lack of patriotism in paying too much homage to German scientists and not enough to Russians. Bazarov likes the Germans because they are scientific and rational, and far superior to the Russians on this count. Each encounter reveals how set and determined both Pavel and Bazarov are. This is about the only quality that they have in common: that is, that each is unbending in his view and each is determined that his way is the correct one.

There has been nothing in Pavel's past life which will enable him to understand Bazarov's point of view. Pavel has always accepted the value of art and music, and when he hears a young man saying that art is meaningless, he practically foams at the mouth with ire. Bazarov doesn't even believe in science as a general principle; only the individual objective experiment is important. Thus, up until now, Bazarov is the complete nihilist who *believes* in absolutely nothing.

Nikolai, like Pavel, is also disturbed, but he does not react as violently against the young people and instead, accepts the fact that the world is changing and that perhaps "the young people are cleverer."

When Bazarov later begins to attack Pavel as useless and aristocratic, Arkady tries to defend Pavel by narrating and explaining his uncle's background. Arkady wants Bazarov to feel some compassion for Pavel, a compassion built upon understanding why Pavel has developed into the type of person he now is. This ability to feel compassion for people and later to enter into wholesome relationships with people is a major point of distinction between Arkady and Bazarov.

Note again how Turgenev interferes in his story by addressing the reader directly, telling him that he will find Pavel's story in the next chapter. Thus, in chapter 6, the main narrative is again interrupted in order to go into the background of one of the characters.

Chapter 7 tells the story of Pavel's life, and we see that he was a dashing young man. Because of a woman, or more accurately, because of a woman's rejection of him, he has suffered a great deal in his earlier life. This information is emphasized because later we will see that Bazarov has the same problem with Madame Odintsova. In fact, the description of the woman Pavel loved is quite similar to that of Madame Odintsova. Both women are enigmatic figures, perfectly pleasant during the day, but wracked with anguish when left to their own thoughts.

After hearing Pavel's story, Bazarov is cynical and ridicules any man who will allow himself to be so dominated by a woman. He has absolutely no sympathy for this type of man, thus the important consideration is that both Pavel and Bazarov have a similar type of experience with a similar type of woman, and both are affected in almost the same way by rejection.

Arkady tries to understand his uncle's position and through this understanding have some type of sympathy for the individual. But Bazarov maintains "that a person who stakes his whole life on the card of a woman's love, then withers and sinks to the point of becoming incapable of anything when that card is trumped—a person like that isn't a man, isn't a male." But ironically, Bazarov will stake almost his entire existence on the love of Madame Odintsova and when rejected will wither away to the point that he cannot work and cannot find himself in life. Arkady, on the contrary, will be seen to have sympathy for both Pavel's and Bazarov's plight. This is a basic difference developing between the two young men.

CHAPTERS 8, 9

Summary

Nikolai and Pavel go to speak to the overseer; Pavel realizes that his brother is not handling the farm correctly but is unable to point out any errors in the management. Even though he has in the past been able to supply money for running the farm, at the present moment he has no extra money to spare and therefore he leaves his brother. Pavel goes to talk to Fenichka, but she is afraid of the cold and distant "aristocratic gentleman."

Pavel wants to see the child and Fenichka goes to bring it. Pavel notes that Fenichka keeps a very neat and orderly house. When she returns with the child, Pavel admires it and Nikolai arrives. Pavel immediately leaves Nikolai, who remembers how he had met his mistress. He had once stopped for an evening at an inn and found it exceptionally well kept and neat. He asked the innkeeper's domestic servant to come and be his housekeeper. The woman agreed and brought her young daughter, Fenichka, with her. After a few years, the woman died of cholera, leaving the young girl alone. Nikolai, who had grown fond of Fenichka, asked her to remain and be his companion.

Meanwhile, Pavel has returned to his study, where he stares at the ceiling "with an almost desperate expression."

The same day, Bazarov also meets Fenichka. He is out in the arbor with Arkady and notices that Fenichka is a very pretty girl. Arkady is pleased for his father's sake, because as Bazarov says, Nikolai is no fool for attaching himself to this girl. Bazarov plays with the child and enjoys it very much.

As Bazarov and Arkady leave, they discuss the miserable condition of the farm. They discuss various views of nature, and Bazarov rejects the romantic conception of nature being a temple, and calls it instead a workshop in which man can work and educate himself. As they approach the house, they hear someone playing Schubert's "Die Erwartung" on the cello, and when Bazarov discovers that it is Nikolai playing it, he bursts out laughing over the incongruous fact of a country farmer in a distant province playing such a piece of classical music.

Commentary

Fenichka's character is developed in these two chapters. Turgenev interrupts the story again in order to give her background, which allows the reader to understand something of the social distinction between her and Nikolai. Fenichka is described in terms of the clean and wholesome Russian peasant, and is in many ways similar to Bazarov's mother in her attention to the basic womanly duties. She is completely subservient to the man who has taken her as his mistress. Perhaps we can say she has yielded with dignity.

The story of Fenichka is presented in contrast to Pavel's story. Thus, we see immediately how far apart the two are. It is at first glance a condescending step for Pavel to go to Fenichka's room, but ultimately, we discover that Pavel is attracted to Fenichka because she bears a strange resemblance to the lady Pavel once loved. Thus, in this chapter we have subtle hints about Pavel's true feelings when Turgenev writes that Pavel looked at Fenichka almost sadly. Fenichka is so simple and basic that she can never perceive Pavel's true feelings and Pavel is too much of a gentleman to reveal them. Thus, later, when Pavel fights the duel with Bazarov, he does so not just to protect his brother's honor, but because he cannot tolerate the idea of Bazarov kissing a woman whom he also admires.

Chapter 8 ends with Pavel sitting alone in his room with his elegant carpets and his distressing loneliness. The description is that of a lost man from the romantic world pathetically clinging to his illusions in an entirely too "real" world.

Bazarov seems to have a natural talent with the peasants and with anyone who cannot contradict his opinions. When he meets

Fenichka and her baby, she allows him to handle the child, but when Arkady tries to handle the baby, it puts up a fight. The touching and "sentimental" scene in which Bazarov idly plays with a child is perhaps intended to give us a hint that even the supremely aloof Bazarov has a hidden spring of tenderness dormant within him. Certainly we can credit Turgenev with subtly preparing us for the breakdown of Bazarov's cold exterior when he is confronted with Madame Odintsova.

Bazarov's nihilism is again revealed when he ridicules Arkady for feeling that Nikolai should marry Fenichka. Arkady actually thought he was being very advanced by advocating such a marriage, but Bazarov is even more advanced or liberal by believing that marriage is just a ridiculous institution that has no meaning. After this discussion, we note a trace of hostility between the friends.

Bazarov is also scornful of the fact that Arkady's father plays classical music on the cello. He finds it highly ridiculous that a forty-four year old father living in a distant Russian province should read classical literature and play classical music.

The reader should now begin to evaluate Bazarov and his views. We should see that Bazarov attacks almost everything about Arkady's family and estate. Basically, he is impolite and intolerant of things in Arkady's family. We should then, be constantly aware of the reactions of each of the young men, both to his own parents and to the other's parents. That is, Arkady could make criticisms later on of the type of people the Bazarovs are, but refrains from doing so. Bazarov makes no effort to conceal his contempt for Arkady's relatives.

At the end of chapter 9, we have another hint that Arkady is not pleased with his friend. After Bazarov has been so critical of Pavel and Nikolai, Arkady feels a slight degree of separation. This will continue until Katya points out at the end that Arkady has finally broken completely from the influence that Bazarov exerted over him.

Summary

After two weeks, everyone except Pavel grew used to the two young men. Pavel, however, came to hate Bazarov "with all the strength of his soul." He regarded Bazarov as arrogant, insolent, and cynical, and suspected that "he all but had contempt for him." The only other person who did not like Bazarov was old Prokofitch who, as a servant, was "just as much an aristocrat as was Pavel."

Arkady and Bazarov often went on long walks and had arguments which Arkady usually lost, even though Bazarov said very little. One day, as they were returning from a walk, Nikolai overheard the two talking when Bazarov was saying that Nikolai is a "very good fellow...but he's on the retired list, his song is sung." Bazarov mentions that Nikolai even reads the poet Pushkin.

Nikolai is so upset by this overheard conversation that he reports it to his brother Pavel. Actually, Nikolai has read constantly in an attempt to keep up with the new generation, and is somewhat disappointed that he is considered so out of date. Furthermore, one day when he was reading a Pushkin poem, his son Arkady came up and gently replaced the book with one by a German entitled *Stoff und Kraft*. Nikolai still remembers his German well enough to read it, but he cannot see any value in this book. Pavel decides that they must have a discussion with Bazarov.

That same day, Pavel had his opportunity to discuss things with Bazarov when the young man referred to a neighbor as a rotter and a petty aristocrat. Pavel objects to both and defends the rights of the aristocrat. Ultimately, after some discussion, Bazarov asks Pavel what benefit he is to mankind, but Pavel merely defends the concept of the aristocrat as a part of the heritage of the world.

After Bazarov tears down all the things that Pavel believes in such as art, poetry, culture, etc., Pavel wonders if nihilism means only to tear down. He asks if "it is necessary to build up." Bazarov explains that it is not their business to build up, but only to "clear the site." Bazarov further explains that the "nihilist" respects no authority and no tradition: he rejects all talk of values as being mere platitudes, and reviles everything.

Pavel wonders how they can tear down when they don't even know why they are destroying. Bazarov explains that "We break things down because we are a force," and a force does not have to "render any account." There is nothing that Bazarov respects; he finds faults with everything. Throughout the discussion, Arkady enthusiastically agrees with his friend. Bazarov ends the discussion by saying that Pavel needs time to think over these things and examine if anything has any value; in the meantime he will continue to dissect frogs.

After they leave, Nikolai reminds his brother that when they were young they thought that their parents were old fashioned, but then admits that he is confident that their values are better than those of the young nihilist.

Commentary

In chapter 10, Turgenev gives us another slant on the character of Bazarov. Note that for all his sarcasm and condescending manner he is basically well liked by all the servants except Prokofitch, who is in his own way "as much an aristocrat as Pavel." Turgenev does not want to present a completely negative picture of Bazarov, but wants the reader to see him as a vividly real person. In terms of literary development, this ability to make his characters into real vivid personalities is one of Turgenev's main contributions to the rise of the realistic novel.

In contrast to many of the realistic techniques, Turgenev also uses a number of devices which smack of the romantic. For example, Nikolai just happens to be situated in a place where he overhears a conversation between Bazarov and Arkady. This technique of an accidentally overheard conversation is artificial and associated with romanticism. From it, Nikolai learns that he is now considered to be "on the retired list." For some fathers, this would be reason enough for complete alienation from the son. The fact that it does not have that effect here allows Arkady and Nikolai ultimately to join together by the end of the novel.

Bazarov had ridiculed Arkady's father for reading Pushkin, so the next time Arkady sees his father reading Pushkin, he replaces it with Buchner's *Stoff und Kraft*. (The book is actually entitled *Kraft und Stoff* [*Force and Matter*] and concerns a materialist view of the world.) The fact that Arkady gives his father this book indicates how much he is still under the control of Bazarov.

Nikolai did try to read the book, and decides that either the contents are rubbish or he is just a stupid man. Since we have seen that Nikolai is cultured (he speaks several languages in addition to knowing classical literature and music), the reader might be led to believe his view that the book *is* so much trash. Pavel's reaction is that Bazarov is being a presumptuous egotist for suggesting this book. This is highly ironic coming from a man who is himself extremely egotistical.

In this chapter, we hear more about the concept of "nihilism." Nikolai and Pavel try to argue that any philosophical concept must have a *positive* end, but Bazarov insists that the "nihilist" is only interested in "clearing the site" by destroying the corruption which presently exists. The older generation cannot understand a concept that stands on totally negative principles. Until all things can be destroyed, the nihilist must revile and undermine all things. They act not for the sake of any values, but merely because they are a force. It does not even matter if they understand why they destroy as long as they *do* destroy. Consequently, there is nothing that the nihilist will respect. The Russian land, country, family, government, church are all equally ridiculous and must be destroyed. What is not brought out in the novel, but is embedded in the concept of "nihilism," is the fact that if "nihilism" were carried to its extreme, it would mean finally that after everything is destroyed, man then must destroy himself. No nihilist can ever build anything because a subsequent adherent of "nihilism" would come along and feel the need to destroy that.

As the discussion between Pavel and Bazarov becomes very heated, Nikolai tries to interpose to prevent a serious disagreement. But there is not much danger of this happening because Bazarov doesn't care enough to get too upset, and Pavel, at this point, feels it would be beneath his aristocratic dignity to become angry with an inferior person. Yet, these types of conflicts prepare us for the approaching duel scene between Bazarov and Pavel.

This chapter also reinforces a wider ranging theme in the novel —the natural antagonism which exists between succeeding generations, between fathers and sons of all periods of history. Nikolai tries to justify his son's different views by reminding Pavel that when they were children, they too thought their parents old fashioned. Basically, Turgenev is suggesting that any two different generations will always fail to understand each other. Pavel, however, only feels that in this particular case the older generation is decidedly the one with truth on its side.

CHAPTER 11

Summary

After the discussion about the "nihilists," Nikolai realizes that despite all his efforts he is more alienated from his son than ever before. He muses on the beauty of nature and poetry and is disappointed that the younger generation has rejected all of this. He dreams of his past happiness and of his wife; he further laments that he can't relive these individual happy moments; that they cannot be extended for an eternal, immortal life.

Suddenly, Fenichka brings him back to reality by calling to him to come to the house. On his way back he meets Pavel who also seems preoccupied. Pavel, not born a romantic, is not capable of dreaming like Nikolai, and thus lives in a more barren world.

The same night, Bazarov suggests that they take up Nikolai's suggestion and go visit Arkady's uncle who is a privy-counselor for a neighboring town. They leave the next day, and "the younger people at Marino were sorry to see them go,...but the elders breathed more easily."

Commentary

Unlike Pavel, who point-blank rejects all the ideas of the younger generation, Nikolai has made some effort to understand the point of view of the young people He did live with them in St. Petersburg and has read what they have read, but he has still failed to understand the modern point of view.

He is trying to see what good can come from their ideas. He wonders if their value can be that they have "fewer traces of feudalism" than the older generation. This is an important point because Nikolai is freeing his serfs and trying to discard the old feudalistic method of managing his land.

Nikolai's final puzzlement is how could the young people reject totally the arts and poetry and all literature. Of course, this would be Turgenev's point of view, since he is creating literature and immediately after having Nikolai query about the nihilist rejection of poetry, Turgenev gives us a magnificently poetic passage describing the area surrounding the arbor. But as we progress in this chapter and as Nikolai loses himself in daydreams about past happiness, Turgenev is slightly critical of Nikolai. If we look closely at Nikolai, we see that he is sadly lacking in the practical sense it takes to run a farm. He needs someone to help him break from the romantic dream world and come to terms with the real world. Thus, Turgenev criticizes both the "nihilist" who rejects everything and the romantic like Nikolai who lives so much in a romantic world that he allows himself to be subdued by the practical considerations of everyday life. His utter romanticism is seen as he ends his reveries with tears in his eyes, and we are reminded of the contrast by the statement that these tears in Bazarov's view would be "a hundred times worse than the cello."

In contrast to Nikolai, the romantic dreamer, Pavel, who was not "a born romantic" in the sentimental sense of the term, is seen as possessing an "exquisitely dry and sensual soul." The comparison leaves Nikolai the more admirable figure of the two.

At the end of the chapter, we see the two young people about to leave Marino to visit Arkady's uncle. Arkady is delighted to do this but "considered it his duty to conceal his feelings. Not for nothing was he a nihilist." Again this gives us a hint that Arkady is not and can never be the true "nihilist."

With the departure from Marino, we have the end of the first cycle of the novel. We now move to a different scene and see the young "nihilists" in other surroundings. The reader should keep in mind a touch of sentimentalism appearing in Bazarov in his reasons for going to visit his parents. And we should also remember Bazarov's relationship with Arkady's father and compare this later with his relationship with his own father.

CHAPTERS 12, 13

Summary

Matvei Ilyich Kolyazin was a vain but good-natured man. He had no particular intellect, but was capable of handling his own affairs. He receives Arkady with good nature and invites him obliquely to a ball that the governor is giving in his honor. Arkady returns to the inn and tells Bazarov, who agrees to meet the governor and "take a look at the gentry." On returning from the governor's house, where they go to pay their respects, they meet Viktor Sitnikov, and old acquaintance of Bazarov's.

Sitnikov suggests that they go and meet a progressive woman named Avdotya Nikitishna Kukshina, who according to Sitnikov, will provide them with a real feast. Bazarov is at first reluctant to go but ultimately agrees to accompany them just out of curiosity.

The three companions arrive at Kukshina's house and are received by the lady who advances the most liberal views. She immediately begins to talk about a variety of typical subjects and demonstrates a superficial knowledge of many contemporary authors and opinions. Throughout the conversation she tries to get Bazarov to agree with her, but he militantly maintains his own individualistic opinions.

Madame Kukshina does mention another person of the neighborhood who shares many of her advanced opinions, a Madame Odintsova, who is a widow and a large landowner. While they are there, a large breakfast is served and with it four bottles of champagne are consumed. After a time, Arkady can stand no more and wants to leave. When the three men are alone, Sitnikov seems proud of having been instrumental in providing his friends with good food and champagne, but his companions give him no credit for his accomplishment.

Commentary

Chapters 12 and 13 function essentially as transitional chapters. Turgenev takes the opportunity to satirize the Russian official who maintains that he is an advanced liberal, but is in reality as much a despot as any of the older officials are.

The characterization of Sitnikov is also satiric. He is the psuedo-intellectual who attaches himself to the fringe of any movement which seems advanced. He is an "idea-taster." He does not comprehend the movement but acts as a parasite so as to gain the attention of people obviously greater than he. In the final chapter, we hear that this absurd person is trying to continue Bazarov's "work" after the latter's death.

Kukshina is also satirized as the advanced and liberated woman. The most cutting remark about her is in the next chapter when she appears at the ball dressed in soiled gloves and dances after everyone else has departed. Kukshina and Sitnikov seem to remain with one another out of desperation in trying to find other companions.

Kukshina's attempt to show off her knowledge of all the contemporary writers in Europe and America indicates the superficiality of her knowledge, since she apparently has not penetrated beneath the surface level of any of these authors.

CHAPTER 14

Summary

At the governor's ball, Arkady's uncle shines like a true French courtier—amiable to all present and especially favorable to the ladies. Endless swarms of people dance and many speak an affected French. Kukshina arrives, but is not appropriately dressed, her gloves being dirty and her dress extremely disheveled.

Suddenly Sitnikov stops and announces the arrival of Odintsova to Arkady, who is immediately impressed and wants to meet her. When introduced, Odintsova acknowledges that she has seen Arkady's father and has heard about him. He becomes completely enraptured with her and chatters on as though he were a stage-struck school boy. She asks him who his companion is, and he rhapsodizes about Bazarov. His enthusiasm for Bazarov moves Madame Odintsova to express her wish to meet the friend. Arkady promises to come for a visit and bring Bazarov with him.

Arkady speaks to Bazarov about Odintsova, but his companion is very cynical about this grand lady. Bazarov's sarcasm annoys Arkady. Kukshina is also annoyed because no one paid any attention to her. The ball ended at four a.m. with Sitnikov and Kukshina dancing a polka-mazurka.

Commentary

Chapter 14 serves to introduce the reader to Madame Odintsova and to satirize the type of provincial Russian ball where the participants ape western culture by their mannerisms and affected French.

The first appearance of Madame Odintsova emphasizes her physical attractiveness. "She carried her bare arms beautifully to set off her graceful figure." Since Bazarov will at first be attracted only by her bodily attributes, it is apropos that Turgenev introduces her with emphasis on her physical beauty. The other quality emphasized is her coldness and severity. Arkady is immediately attracted to her and wonders if she dances. Vaguely, it is suggested that dancing is not an art which a nihilist would practice, and Bazarov does not participate in any of the dances. But when Arkady asks Madame Odintsova *if* she dances, he is unconsciously associating her with the nihilist viewpoint which is opposed to dancing, but she thinks that he is referring to her age.

At the end of the chapter, Bazarov tries to cover up his attraction for Madame Odintsova by saying derogatory things about her and by emphasizing how attractive her body is.

CHAPTER 15

Summary

Bazarov agrees to call upon Madame Odintsova at her hotel. When they are admitted to her rooms, they find that she is dressed very simply in a morning frock. Arkady introduces his friend and secretly notices that Bazarov is embarrassed in the presence of this beautiful aristocratic woman. Even Bazarov is annoyed to find himself "afraid of a woman."

Anna Sergeyevna Odintsova is the daughter of a landowner who educated his daughter in the best way possible and when he died left her only a small estate to manage for herself. A very rich man somewhat older than she saw her and asked for her hand in marriage. She accepted and when he died six years later, she became an immensely wealthy woman. She traveled a good deal throughout Europe, but finally returned to settle in Russia. She was not liked in the province, since she has always been somewhat distant. In fact, there was quite a bit of nasty gossip about her.

When she meets Bazarov, she expresses her delight in knowing a person "who has the courage not to believe in anything." Whenever she brings up a subject for discussion which Bazarov does not like, she immediately changes to some other topic which suits him. As they are leaving, she extends both of them an invitation to visit her at her estate. Both agree to come, even though Bazarov pretends indifference.

After they leave, Bazarov shocks Arkady by emphasizing only the physical beauty of Madame Odintsova. Two days later they leave for her home, Nikolskoe. Bazarov mentions that it is his "day of my angel" and explains that his parents are expecting him but they will have to wait a while longer.

Commentary

For the first time, we see Bazarov in a situation where he is uncomfortable. He is in the presence of a person who has a personality as strong as his own and this disconcerts him. Formerly every time we have seen him he was in control of the situation by being coldly aloof and austere, but here Madame Odintsova is the cold and withdrawn one. She seems to be the controlling factor, not Bazarov.

We must also remember that Madame Odintsova is somewhat older than either Arkady or Bazarov, and she has lived more extensively then either student. Arkady is astounded as he for the first time notices a form of contradiction in his friend; Arkady is shocked to see Bazarov in a situation where he blushes. As they leave, to cover up his embarrassment, Bazarov again returns to the subject of Madame Odintsova's beautiful body. He feels on safer ground talking about a woman's anatomy and even wishes, ironically and ridiculously, that he had her body in the dissecting room.

This chapter follows Turgenev's technique of interrupting the narrative to give some background information about a character. We learn that Madame Odintsova has lived a varied life filled with many experiences and finally decided to return to this Russian province to settle down. Furthermore, we hear that she is not liked by the other people. This causes Bazarov later to ask her if she is disturbed by the rumors in the town.

CHAPTER 16

Summary

Arkady and Bazarov are received in the very stately home of Madame Odintsova. When they are alone, Bazarov remarks very curtly that Madame Odintsova is a duchess who is condescending to receive a future doctor or a doctor's son; he feels that she is simply indulging in a whim.

At tea, they learn that Madame Odintsova lives with her aunt and sister. The aunt is an elderly noblewoman tolerated mainly because of her high birth. The sister is a shy girl of eighteen. Madame Odintsova suggests to Bazarov that they argue about something. He calls to her attention a book of some drawings of Switzerland and explains that he is interested only in the geological aspect of the sketches. She wonders how he can get along in life without any artistic appreciation and asks if he doesn't want to understand people. He replies that "people are trees in a forest; no botanist would study every individual birch tree." Furthermore, the difference between a clever and a stupid person is the same as that between a healthy and sick person. If one could reform society, there would be no cause for sickness.

Odintsova asks Arkady what he thinks of these ideas, and Arkady obsequiously agrees with all that Bazarov has said. The aunt arrives and we *do* see that she is just tolerated by everyone. In fact, no one pays any attention to her except to adhere to the proper obeisances. Porfiry Platonovitch, a neighbor to Odintsova, arrives to play cards. While they are playing, Odintsova suggests that Arkady accompany her sister Katya to the piano. Arkady feels slighted because he senses that Madame Odintsova is dismissing him.

As Katya plays, he is struck by the beauty of Mozart's music despite his feelings of anti-romanticism and his advocation of nihilism. Arkady asks her to explain why she chose this particular piece of music, and Katya, naturally reticent, fails to respond to the question.

Odintsova suggests that Bazarov take her for a walk in order to teach her the Latin names for the various field plants. When he wants to know why she feels the need to know the Latin names, she replies that "one must have order in everything."

Bazarov and Arkady alone at night discuss the two sisters. Arkady praises Madame Odintsova, while Bazarov points out that the real marvel is not the Madame but Katya. That same night, Madame Odintsova is also thinking about her guests. She is intrigued by Bazarov and is fascinated by the sharpness of his opinions. Furthermore, she is confused by her own ambiguous feelings.

The next morning, Madame Odintsova and Bazarov go off to study botany while Arkady remains at home with Katya. When they return, Bavarov greets Arkady "as though they hadn't seen each other that day."

Commentary

When Bazarov and Arkady arrive at Madame Odintsova's estate, she immediately notes the difference between the two men by promising music as entertainment to Arkady while observing that Bazarov would not be tempted by such entertainment. Again, we note that there is an essential difference between the two friends in that Arkady does care for many of the things which the "nihilists" and Bazarov depreciate.

Madame Odintsova openly wants Bazarov to tell her some of his ideas. She wonders how Bazarov can get along without an appreciation of art. He explains that he was looking at some pictures of Switzerland not for the romantic scenery but instead for the geological structure of the land. Madame Odintsova feels that one must have an artistic nature in order to understand people, but Bazarov feels that "individual personalities are not worth the trouble." "People are like trees in the forest; no botanist will stop to study every birch separately." What Bazarov fails to understand is that a botanist *would* indeed study the various types of trees (birch, elm, oak, etc.) and would also be interested in the differentiating characteristics among each separate birch tree, or oak tree, etc. To suggest that all people are the same as every birch tree is the same as an employment of a shoddy analogy and exhibits a gross misunderstanding of human nature.

Madame Odintsova makes the separation between the four people. She sends Arkady to sit with Katya and listen to the piano while she and Bazarov argue. He is struck by the piano music even though a true nihilist would not be. Thus, he is like his father and has inherited from Nikolai an appreciation of music. This mutual appreciation of music will bring Katya and Arkady together more and more until they become engaged.

One of the great contrasts between Madame Odintsova and Bazarov is her emphasis on order. She says that man must "have order in everything." Without order life would be too erratic and too boring. She even wants to know the Latin names for the various plants because these names indicate to her a degree of order. The "nihilist," however, is out to destroy all existing order and to replace it with a type of dominant anarchy. It is significant that Bazarov becomes attracted to a person who believes something diametrically opposed to his way of thinking and, furthermore, to someone whose way of life prevails over him while he remains at Nikolskoe. Later, he even admits that without the order found in Madame Odintsova's house the visit would not have been prolonged so long. The order, in other words, did contribute to the pleasure of their visit.

Madame Odintsova is also attracted to Bazarov because he is so different from her. She is troubled by her own feelings because she has lived for such a long time in an ordered world and here is a person who exudes a certain amount of ambiguity. For her, he represents a degree of disorder entering into her otherwise ordered existence. The reader should be aware of just how far she will allow her sense of order to be violated *before she draws back*.

CHAPTER 17

Summary

Arkady and Bazarov spend a very pleasant two weeks in the "orderly household" of Madame Odintsova. Bazarov at first complains that this strictly regulated existence violates his sense of democracy. Madame Odintsova parries that without order in a country life one would be conquered by boredom.

Apparently unrequited in his feelings for Madame Odintsova, Arkady seeks consolation by spending his time with the young Katya. The two young people play the piano, read stories together, and observe nature, but Arkady is determined that no sentimental emotions will influence him.

Meanwhile Bazarov is maddened by the strange feelings he has toward Madame Odintsova because he realizes that he is totally unable to subdue these emotions. At the same time, Bazarov occupies Madame Odintsova's thoughts constantly. While Bazarov is contemplating his relationship with Madame Odintsova and realizing the futility of it, his father's old retainer, Timofeich, drops by for a visit. Bazarov wonders if his parents have sent the retainer and sends word that he will soon be home for a visit.

That evening, Bazarov surprises Madame Odintsova by announcing his intentions of leaving soon. She recalls to him that he has promised to teach her some chemistry and help her in other pursuits. She assures him that he will be missed and that she will be quite bored when he leaves. Bazarov sarcastically suggests that she can return to her ordered and quiet life and will not be affected by the departure of such an insignificant person. Upon further entreaties, Bazarov asks Madame Odintsova why a woman with "your intelligence, with your beauty," lives in the country. She makes some observations about her life and assures her new friend that she is very unhappy. She has lived so much in the world that she no longer finds many things to interest her. She wishes that she could actually get strongly attached to something, and Bazarov counters by telling her that she is incapable of falling in love. Secretly, he thinks that she is being flirtatious at this moment and is quite disturbed. As Bazarov prepares to leave, she tries to restrain him, but he presses her hand rather hard and quickly leaves.

After his departure, Madame Odintsova sat for a long time before she went to bed. Bazarov, however, walked for two hours before he went to bed. Arkady tries to question his friend about his whereabouts, but becomes so emotionally disturbed that he cannot speak clearly.

Commentary

Note that Bazarov has finally let his guard drop and he is affected by something outside of himself. Anxiety begins to appear and he changes significantly. This is one of the most crucial chapters of the novel because Bazarov's inner nature conflicts with his intellectual nature for the first time. Love in the romantic sense has always been mere tomfoolery to him, but now he seems captured by Odintsova. He lacked the "strength to turn his back on her."

The two pairs of lovers almost seem star-crossed. Arkady thinks that he is in love with Odintsova but more and more he is attracted by Katya's charm. Arkady is as yet still unaware of many things about himself. "Without noticing or confessing to himself that such nonsense interests him too," he is aroused or affected somewhat by the music, poetry, etc. Furthermore, he thinks that he is in love with Madame Odintsova, but feels uncomfortable in her presence. On the contrary, he is quite at ease with Katya.

Intellectually, Bazarov still continues to fight any feelings of love. He still believes that "love in the ideal sense, or, as he expressed it, the romantic sense, was nonsense — an unforgivable stupidity." But nevertheless, "his blood began to burn as soon as he thought of her." His change is even noticed by Arkady, who begins to lose faith in his friend. He noticed that Bazarov spoke more reluctantly, and often looked angry and more than anything else, Bazarov fidgeted and looked ill at ease. Bazarov had always maintained that "If you take a fancy to a woman, try to gain your end or leave her." But with Madame Odintsova, he knows that he can never gain his end, and yet he can't leave her either. Thus, as noted earlier, he is trapped in love in the same way as was Pavel, but the difference between them is that Bazarov condemns himself later almost as much as he condemned Pavel. His failure to see the similarities in the situations is perhaps a flaw in his character.

The more human aspect of Bazarov's nature is seen when the old Bazarov servant comes to inquire about him. Bazarov dismisses the servant as soon as possible, but nevertheless, we see that he is affected by the desires of his parents. If Arkady had shown the same desire to respect the wishes of his parents, Bazarov would have criticized him severely. Thus, gradually, we note more and more of a change in the nihilist.

Philosophically, according to nihilism, Bazarov should be the person who can live totally alone, without dependence on another person. Yet in this chapter, we see that it is more Madame Odintsova who can and who will be able to live without love or human companionship. Suddenly, we realize that in this respect, she is more the nihilist than "Mr. Nihilist" himself, who craves the company and love of Madame Odintsova. But at the same time, her life is also similar to that of Pavel's because she has indeed experienced so many things in the past and has traveled and done so many things that she expects no new adventure. But Bazarov philosophically believes that there is no such thing as a new experience in the same way that he believes that there is no *new* birch tree.

The breach between Arkady and Bazarov is heightened at the end of the chapter as their separation is caused by the two ladies. Arkady is still jealous of the time that Madame Odintsova spends with Bazarov, even though he thoroughly enjoys the hours he spends with Katya.

CHAPTER 18

Summary

The following day, the entire group chooses to remain in the parlor because it is raining outside. Madame Odintsova asks Bazarov to come to the study to point out the chemistry book he had previously suggested she read. Actually, she wants to resume the conversation which was so abruptly broken off the night before.

She tries to discuss happiness and one's purpose in life with Bazarov, but he finds difficulty in discussing such things. "I am not generally accustomed to discussing my feelings and there is such a distance between us." Odintsova presses Bazarov until he is forced to admit what is really happening inside him. She is stunned when he tells her that he is "madly and foolishly" in love with her. When he grabs her and holds her to his chest, she breaks away in complete amazement. The confused Bazarov hurriedly rushes from the room.

Shortly afterward, Bazarov sends her a note requesting permission to stay one more day before he leaves for his visit with his parents. She answers that it is not necessary to go away because the two have not understood each other. Madame Odintsova did not understand her own reaction but thinks that "peace is still the best thing in the world."

Commentary

Madame Odintsova had earlier said that she doesn't know what she wants, and in these chapters seems to be leading Bazarov on to find out his true feelings. It could easily appear and be interpreted that she is acting as a coquette would by suggesting to Bazarov things that she does not mean. But the central point is that she is not content and does not know how to find any type of fulfillment. Thus, she questions Bazarov—the man who has dared not to believe in anything—about his inner feelings in order to try to understand some aspect of her own feelings.

Consequently when Bazarov makes his impassioned declaration of love, Madame Odintsova is entirely taken aback. She was simply not prepared for this. In other words, she has lived an ordered life and is essentially a very self-centered person. She has suffered hardship and has undergone many difficulties; she has now found comfort and does not want to give herself to any person who might interfere with the sense of order and security she now enjoys. After he leaves, she decides that she should not trifle with any commitment because "peace is still the best thing in the world."

In contrast, Bazarov's declaration affects him deeply. It was not something he could easily do. After he declares his love he is visibly affected. "He was gasping; his whole body was visibly trembling.... It was passion struggling inside him, strong and tragic." Thus, Bazarov undergoes a greater change than does Madame Odintsova and consequently violates his entire philosophy of "nihilism."

CHAPTER 19

Summary

Madame Odintsova felt so awkward about her scene with Bazarov that when her neighbor, Porfiry Platonovitch, arrived for cards, she felt greatly relieved. When Bazarov is able to speak to his hostess alone, he explains that now he must leave: there is only one condition which would allow him to remain, and that could never be.

Madame Odintsova feels afraid of herself and of Bazarov, and keeps her sister close to her all day until Sitnikov makes a sudden appearance. Under other circumstances, he would not have been so well received, but he is able to relieve some of the tension.

That night, Bazarov tells Arkady that he plans to leave and Arkady announces his intention of returning to Marino. Before going to sleep, Arkady realizes that he will miss Madame Odintsova, but subconsciously he is more concerned about Katya.

The next morning, Sitnikov offers to let Arkady ride with him so that Bazarov can have the smaller vehicle. After farewells are made in which Madame Odintsova asserts her determination to meet Bazarov again, Arkady leaves with Sitnikov. When they come to the crossroads where they must part, Arkady changes his mind and asks Bazarov for permission to go with him. He leaves Sitnikov, who is confused by this sudden reversal.

In the carriage, Bazarov is very cynical about women and feels that no man should allow a woman to get the best of him. Yet, he feels as though he has "been thrashed" by a woman. By the time Bazarov is through railing against women, they have arrived at his father's house.

Commentary

The change in Bazarov is further emphasized by the fact that he immediately apologizes to Madame Odintsova for his earlier actions. He would never have apologized to anyone for anything at Marino. Consequently, both Bazarov and Arkady are changing, but the significant difference is that Arkady's change is simply a reversion to his basic nature and Bazarov is changing against his intellectual convictions or nature. When he announces his intentions to leave, he explains that it is because he knows that Odintsova does not love him and never can. Thus, the Bazarov who ridiculed Pavel for such romantic nonsense as love is now a victim of the same passion. Madame Odintsova can say nothing to this declaration and only thinks that she is "afraid of this man" because he might destroy her sense of order. We should also remember that in the end Madame Odintsova does make a marriage of convenience—one that will not effect the order she has established for herself.

The arrival of Sitnikov serves to alleviate a delicate situation. He acts as a buffer to many warring emotions. Besides the tension between Bazarov and Madame Odintsova, Arkady and Bazarov are becoming less friendly. "For some time past a hypocritically free and easy bantering had been going on between the two young men, a trick that always indicates secret dissatisfaction or unexpressed suspicions." The difference between the young friends is again emphasized when Arkady decides temporarily not to visit Bazarov's family because "I'm afraid of making them, and you, feel awkward." Yet, Bazarov intentionally made Arkady's family feel awkward. In this comparison, we see that Arkady, in spite of his attempts at "nihilism," is still basically a more humane and tactful individual.

The two friends are not yet ready to part company. The presence of Sitnikov makes Arkady realize that there is much more value in the friendship with Bazarov than in the acquaintance with Sitnikov. Thus, on the spur of the moment, Arkady decides to accompany his friend to the Bazarov home. During the trip Bazarov's frustration is indicated by the cynical remarks he makes about man becoming the slave of a woman only if he is an educated man. The peasants beat their wives and are happy, but the intelligent man is always defeated (or beaten) by a lady.

CHAPTER 20

Summary

As the two friends step down from the coach, Vassily Ivanovitch Bazarov and his wife Arina Vlassevna smother their son with kisses and embraces. The mother is so overjoyed at seeing her son for the first time in three years that she can hardly control herself. The father tries to calm her so as not to make Bazarov feel uncomfortable. Arkady is introduced to the parents and taken to his room in the "humble military home." Vassily Ivanovitch is very apologetic about the house, but Bazarov thinks this is affected and explains that they are not nobility but only good simple people.

Bazarov's father tries to impress his son by relating his attempts at reform on the farm and by expressing an interest in the latest scientific and medical discoveries. He explains that he no longer practices medicine, but he does give free advice and often administers to the peasants. Arina Vlassevna treats the two young men to a magnificent feast accompanied with champagne.

When they retire for the night, Vassily Ivanovitch comes to speak with Bazarov, but his son dismisses him because of his preoccupation with his recent experiences with Madame Odintsova.

"Arina Vlassevna was a true lady of the olden days; she should have lived two hundred years ago in the days of old Moscow." She is a very kind, devout, simple, and superstitious woman who dotes upon her son.

Commentary

Bazarov makes everyone feel uncomfortable except Madame Odintsova. Even Bazarov's parents feel intimidated by their son, who apparently cares very little about how sensitive they are. Bazarov comments about his own father in the same way that he commented about Nikolai. He scorns his own father in almost the same way that he laughed at Nikolai. Both fathers have attempted to keep up with modern developments and Bazarov cannot appreciate the efforts. Bazarov's father mentions some medical theories that he has recently read, but Bazarov says that he scorns all medical theories and pays no attention to any authority. Of course, part of his behavior toward his parents may be due to his disappointment with himself as a result of his unrequited love for Madame Odintsova.

Bazarov's mother is similar to Fenichka, that is, the old Russian who is concerned with the household and with looking after her husband. She is ripe with superstition and peasant customs and her sole concern is keeping her family happy. Sadly, Turgenev notes that "Such women are disappearing now. God knows whether one should rejoice over that."

CHAPTER 21

Summary

On arising the next morning, Arkady saw Vassily Ivanovitch working in the garden. The father is anxious to hear as much about his son as he can. Arkady tells Vassily Ivanovitch that Bazarov is "one of the most remarkable people" he has ever known.

Furthermore, he is confident that "a great future awaits" Bazarov in some way. He then tells the history of their meeting and friendship. Vassily Ivanovitch knows that Bazarov does not like a great show of feelings and suggests that they try not to interfere with him too much. Bazarov appears just in time to join them for breakfast and to advise his father about a patient who is suffering from jaundice.

At noon, Arkady and Bazarov are stretched out in the shadow of a small haystack. Bazarov tells something of his earlier life and affirms that his parents have been very good to him. He is pleased that his folks have been able to adjust so well to their old age, but for himself, he feels so insignificant in view of all eternity. He feels very bitter about life and is still suffering something of the self-humiliation resultant from his defeat by a woman. Arkady, not knowing about Bazarov's relationship with Madame Odintsova, cannot understand his friend who continues to be extremely cynical and negative. They disagree on several subjects, particularly whether a man should have any principles or not.

Just as the argument is about to get out of hand, Arkady suggests that they take a nap. A little later, Arkady makes an observation about a dry maple leaf resembling a butterfly in flight. Bazarov tells Arkady not to talk so foolishly, and asserts that Arkady seems determined to follow in the footsteps of his idiot uncle. Arkady feels that this is an insult that he cannot tolerate, but Bazarov does not stop. He goads Arkady further by sarcastically stating that only a stupid man feels the need to defend his family. Arkady wants to stop the discussion before they quarrel too seriously. Bazarov, however, would like to have one good quarrel "to the death, to annihilation." He suggests that he could seize Arkady's throat and destroy him. At this moment, the fight is prevented by the lucky appearance of Vassily Ivanovitch. The father explains that a local priest is going to dine with them, and since he knows his son's anti-clerical views, he hopes that he will not be offended by the priest. Bazarov asserts that he does not object so long as the priest does not eat his share of the food.

That night after supper, the group played cards and the priest proceeded to win some money from Bazarov. During the course of the evening, Bazarov's mother sat solicitously beside him offering him various things to drink.

The next day Bazarov announces his intentions to leave because he is bored and can't get any work done. He wants to go back to Marino, where he can at least accomplish something. Vassily Ivanovitch is greatly disappointed, but does not dare question or rebuke his son. After his son leaves, he is comforted by his wife in the loss.

Commentary

Whereas Bazarov was abrupt and critical of both Arkady's and his own parents, Arkady conforms to his true nature and is exceptionally considerate of the Bazarovs. He is polite to the old man and takes delight in talking with Bazarov's mother. He discusses their son with them and makes him out to be a greater person than Bazarov actually is. It is, however, highly ironic that Arkady says that Bazarov is "hostile to all effusive feelings," since his friend has just been very effusive with Madame Odintsova. Arkady tells Vassily Bazarov that his son is destined to become a great man some day. This comment is additionally ironic in view of the fact that Bazarov will soon be dead.

The scene between the two friends offers additional views of Bazarov. He is still feeling humiliated for expressing his inner feelings to Madame Odintsova and speaks with extreme malice and hatred. He attacks Arkady relentlessly and mentions the *reductio ad absurdum* of the nihilist theory: "Having decided to mow everything down, then mow yourself down too." Also, he is ready to fight with his friend "to the death, to annihilation." The fight with all its portending viciousness is interrupted by the appearance of Bazarov's father, but at the moment he appeared, Bazarov was indeed ready to destroy his friend totally. Ironically, Vassily Ivanovitch immediately admires the physical appearance of the two young people and comments about how much strength is in each one, but does not know that this same strength was about to be used to destroy each of them.

Summary

The two friends leave the next day, and instead of going to Fyodot's, they follow an impulse and go to Madame Odintsova's, even though they both know that they are indulging in a bit of "foolishness." They realize the impropriety of their actions when they arrive and find Madame Odintsova somewhat cold and nonreceptive to their sudden return visit.

Arkady realizes that he had wanted to see Katya as much as he had wanted to see Madame Odintsova, but the younger sister never emerged from her room during the entire day. They leave Nikolskoe and return to Marino, where they are received with open arms.

Things have not been going well for Nikolai: the hired laborers are giving him trouble, the new machinery has proved ineffective, and the peasants are squabbling among themselves. All Pavel can do is to admonish his brother to remain calm at all costs. Arkady is sympathetic, and Bazarov chooses not to get involved with any of the family problems.

Arkady thinks about Nikolskoe constantly and is surprised to find that he feels bored under the same roof with Bazarov. Under the pretext of studying the organization of Sunday schools in the area, he gallops off to Madame Odintsova's. He is delighted that the first person he meets is Katya, and soon overcomes his uneasiness when Madame Odintsova greets him rather warmly.

Commentary

The opening scene is somewhat comic when we consider that these two are supposed to be adult and intellectual "nihilists." Both of them realize that in terms of their code they are being foolish in even considering a return visit to Madame Odintsova's. As they hedge the question they appear more like two immature school boys than adults, and the decision is finally just a whim which both later regret. Arkady finally makes the decision, and as he does so, he is suddenly aware that he wants to see Katya as much as he ever wanted to see Madame Odintsova. This is for him a momentous step in separating himself from Bazarov.

Important in this chapter is the ineffective romantic who cannot manage to control his help and allows the farm to deteriorate. All the "aristocratic" Pavel can do is say, *"Du calme! Du calme!"* Nikolai simply does not know how to manage the farm, and Pavel is too wrapped up in his own little world. Bazarov is also seen as an ineffective person because he refuses to become involved in any of the problems. The hope lies with Arkady, who assimilates the romantic and the practical, the ideal and the real.

Symbolically at the end of the chapter, Arkady strikes off on his own for the first time. Never before could he have conceived of being bored under the same roof as Bazarov, but now, he is beginning to establish his own identity and he returns to Nikolskoe, not to see Madame Odintsova but to find Katya.

CHAPTER 23

Summary

After Arkady leaves, Bazarov is possessed by a fever to work on his experiments. Except for a few brief clashes, Pavel and Bazarov are able to avoid each other. Both Nikolai and Pavel do take pleasure in observing the young man in his laboratory. The only person at Marino who Bazarov really responds to and gets along with is Fenichka. Fenichka likewise responds to Bazarov. Perhaps it is because she does not consider him of noble birth and could therefore feel more at ease around him.

One day as Bazarov was returning from a walk, he found Fenichka sitting on a bench in a secluded part of the arbor. She thinks that the heat is making her sick, but after Bazarov takes her pulse, he announces that she shall live to be a hundred. They laugh and talk together about his studying and his occupation. She later tells him that the drops he had given her earlier for the baby were very beneficial. Bazarov jokingly said that he has to be paid, but he doesn't want money. He asks for one of her roses. As they are joking, Fenichka thinks she hears Pavel in the vicinity. She expresses her fear and dislike for the man. Bazarov then jokes with her some more and tells her to smell the rose. He leans forward to smell it with her and uses this opportunity to kiss her fully on her parted lips. At this moment, Pavel appears and greets them. Fenichka runs away immediately, and after Pavel leaves, he walks for a long time before he returns to the house in a highly disturbed state of mind.

Commentary

Bazarov is still attempting to forget his unrequited love by devoting himself to work: "he was possessed with a fever to work." Also, we see in the first part of the chapter how much Pavel continues to despise the young "nihilist."

This chapter presents Bazarov as a most likable and most human person by his conversation and relationship with the honest and simple Fenichka. She feels very comfortable in his presence "because she unconsciously felt that Bazarov lacked all the qualities of a nobleman, lacked all the superiority that both attracts and repels." There is a common bond of friendship developing between them and through this relationship, we see more into the essential nature of Bazarov than we did when he was discussing things with Madame Odintsova. He does possess a type of natural charm and easy manner with Fenichka. Furthermore, after his disappointing attempts to find love with Madame Odintsova, he is able to become attracted more easily to Fenichka's simple but sincere charms.

The fact that Pavel saw the two kissing prepares the reader for Pavel's insistence upon a duel in the next chapter. The difference between the two men is seen in the fact that Fenichka reacts strongly to Bazarov but when Pavel appears, she freezes into almost immobility. Pavel, however, will be gentleman enough never to tell Nikolai that he saw Bazarov kissing Fenichka.

CHAPTER 24

Summary

Two hours later, Pavel calls on Bazarov and asks about the latter's views on dueling. Bazarov says that theoretically duels are

absurd, but that they can serve a practical purpose. Much to Bazarov's amazement, Pavel challenges him to a duel for the ostensible
reason that he finds Bazarov detestable and superfluous at Marino.
They agree to fight with pistols at eight paces and without benefit
of seconds at six a.m. the next day. Bazarov insists that they have
a witness and suggests Nikolai's valet, Piotr, who "stands at the
peak of civilization" for the role. Once Pavel leaves, Bazarov laughs
to himself about the idiocy of the entire affair, about the meaningless kiss he gave Fenichka, and Pavel's asinine gallantry. "What a
comedy we played," he muses, "like trained dogs dancing on their
hind legs."

Bazarov starts a letter to his parents, but tears it up thinking
that if something happens to him, they will hear about it soon enough.
He finally decides that nothing is going to happen to him anyway.
He goes in search of Piotr and tells him to report to him early the
next morning for some urgent business. That night he has many
strange dreams concerning himself, Madame Odintsova, Pavel, and
Fenichka.

Piotr wakes them up at four and they leave for the dueling
place. Piotr is frightened when he learns the true purpose of the
trip. Bazarov sees some workers who are also up this early and feels
how useless his trip is compared to the workers who are going to do
something worthwhile.

Up to the last minute, Bazarov jokes about Piotr's abject fear
and the absurdity of the entire episode. But Pavel is in the deepest
earnest about the duel. Pavel fires and the bullet barely grazes
Bazarov's ear. He returns the shot and hits Pavel in the thigh. When
Pavel reminds Bazarov that each is entitled to another shot, Bazarov dismisses him and assumes the role of the doctor tending to
Pavel's wound.

Bazarov must first calm Piotr in order to send him to the
house after help. Pavel is impressed with Bazarov's honorable actions. Piotr returns with Nikolai, who is dreadfully upset. Pavel gal-
lantly assumes full responsibility for the duel and insists that he
insulted Bazarov in such a way that Bazarov was forced to fight.

Later, the household is totally disrupted, and Fenichka makes every possible attempt to avoid Bazarov. Nikolai apologizes for Pavel's action, but he never discovers the real cause of the duel. Bazarov stifles Pavel's attempts to be magnanimous and as he departs, he calls back "damned feudalists," over his shoulder.

While Pavel is convalescing, there is a great deal of tension in the house. Fenichka can hardly face Pavel, and only the old retainer, Prokofitch, who remembered duels from the old days, is not disturbed by the event. Pavel finally calls Fenichka to his room and asks her if she feels no guilt about what she has done. Fenichka answers that it was not her fault and that she could not stop Bazarov from doing what he did. She maintains that she loves Nikolai very much and would die immediately if he thought she was unfaithful. At this point, Nikolai enters and is surprised and pleased when Fenichka openly throws herself into his arms.

After Fenichka leaves the room, Pavel tells his brother that he should do his duty to Fenichka by marrying her and making their relationship decent. Nikolai is astonished at his brother whom he has "always considered the most inflexible opponent of such marriages." Nikolai is overjoyed at this change in Pavel and warmly embraces his brother.

Left alone, Pavel's eyes are moist and he decides that he must go away as soon as he regains his health. "Illuminated by the glaring daylight, his handsome, gaunt head lay on the white pillow like the head of a dead man — and he was, in effect, a dead man."

Commentary

This chapter presents the duel between Bazarov and Pavel. It should be noted that some months earlier, Bazarov would never have consented to the duel. Because it implies standing up for one's honor or principles a duel is in direct opposition to anything a nihilist could advocate. Besides this, dueling for the sake of honor is the height of romanticism. Bazarov, then, accepts out of a sense of boredom and disquiet. However, he does refuse to go so far as to carry a letter in his pocket blaming himself, because "it is just a little like a French romance." As an alternative, he suggests using Piotr.

Thus, we see now why Turgenev has emphasized that Piotr is the emancipated servant because only as such could he possibly function in the role of a witness. Note also that after Pavel leaves, Bazarov admits how foolish it all was, but feels that under the circumstances, it was impossible to refuse Pavel. Furthermore, he knows that the cause of the duel resulted from the fact that he was seen kissing Fenichka. For a "nihilist," this reason only adds to the absurdity of the event.

The next day, Piotr proves not to be as "emancipated" as he thought himself: the duel virtually terrifies him. While waiting, Bazarov, who has always emphasized the value of the practical in life, notices that some other men are up that early, but acknowledges that the others are going to some useful employment. Again, he feels the incongruity of his actions and his views.

After Pavel is wounded slightly, he tries to maintain the right for Bazarov to shoot again as was earlier agreed upon. Bazarov refuses and assumes the role of doctor. For the first time, Pavel realizes that a man as different from him as Bazarov can still be an honorable man. He is now impressed with what an honorable person Bazarov is. It is ironic that Bazarov had to participate in something so romantic and so alien to his beliefs as a duel before Pavel could see any worthy quality in him. That is, Bazarov had to perform something in Pavel's world before Pavel could evaluate Bazarov's importance.

Bazarov's main regret about the duel is that his work is now interrupted, and he expresses his disgust when he leaves by referring to the entire household as "damned feudalists." After he leaves, Pavel calls Nikolai to insist that he do "the right thing" and marry Fenichka. This move is made not because he has shifted from his aristocratic ideas of the impropriety of such a marriage, but because he is probably in love with Fenichka, and knows that she loves only Nikolai. He then is left alone without even the ability to dream. It was as though "Pavel was indeed a corpse."

CHAPTER 25

Summary

At Nikolskoe, Arkady spends all his time in the presence of Katya. He is surprised at first when she mentions how much he has changed and indicates that it is for the better. She suggests that he was too much under Bazarov's influence, and admits that she found Bazarov alien to her personality. She says: "He's a wild animal, and you and I are domesticated." Arkady is impressed with Katya's power of observation and her ability to discern the truth of situations in spite of the fact that she has lived alone so much of her life. She explains that she likes the simple life and wouldn't even want to marry a rich man. Arkady sees that Katya is far superior to her sister and in a moment of excitement tells her that he wouldn't exchange her for anyone in the world, and then he leaves her quickly to conceal his embarrassment.

Returning to his room, he finds Bazarov, who has thus far kept his presence a secret. He tells Arkady about the duel with Pavel; Arkady hears the story out, but feels horrified and ashamed. Bazarov wants to leave immediately because he thinks that Arkady is there only to have an affair with Madame Odintsova. Arkady denies this emphatically, and suggests that the lady would want to see Bazarov.

Madame Odintsova does learn of Bazarov's presence and requests an interview with him. Bazarov immediately explains that he has come to his senses since their last meeting and apologizes for his past stupidities. They forget the past and talk of the present. Bazarov tells her that he is sure Arkady is in love with her, but she thinks that he is mistaken. Arkady, in the meantime, had been sitting alone without the slightest trace of jealousy over the fact that Bazarov was alone with Madame Odintsova.

Commentary

In action and in thought, Arkady's romantic tendencies are now emerging. He is with Katya and is happy that he can express himself in "pretty language" without becoming defensive about it or without being scorned for it.

Katya is now seen to have a certain strength of her own. Previously we had seen that she remained in the background and said or did very little, but now with Arkady, she expresses herself openly and cleverly. These two, the two most admirable characters in the novel, proceed to discuss some of the other characters, especially Odintsova and Bazarov. Katya's keen insight emerges when she evaluates Bazarov as being a "bird of prey" while she characterizes herself and Arkady as "tame." She also notes that her sister values her independence and her "order" too much.

Katya's maturity is seen in her explanation of a woman's role. She maintains that the woman must be able to preserve her self-respect while at the same time being perfectly ready to yield. Odintsova could never yield and could never approach saying anything like this. The older sister's excessive pride would prevent her from ever giving herself completely to another.

Bazarov returns and is still upset over the trouble he had previously had with Madame Odintsova. In this scene between the two young friends, Bazarov is more hostile than he has ever been. This is because he thinks that Arkady actually came to see Madame Odintsova and is jealous. Furthermore, it shows the growing dissatisfaction that the two friends feel toward each other.

Bazarov sums up their relationship as follows: "A romantic would say: I feel that our paths are beginning to divide but I simply say that we have grown tired of each other." From Arkady's viewpoint, this is a good change because we know that Arkady's true nature cannot emerge as long as he is under Bazarov's influence. Arkady's complete change is noted in the last sentence when he realizes that Madame Odintsova is sitting with Bazarov and he feels no quirk of jealousy. In other words, Arkady has now found his love with Katya and is no longer concerned with the older lady.

CHAPTER 26

Summary

The day after Bazarov's arrival, Arkady and Katya are sitting alone in the garden. He tries to tell her how much he has changed and credits her with being a good influence upon him. He wants to tell her something that will surprise her, but he gets twisted up in his speech so badly that Katya has to tell him that she does not know what he is trying to say.

At this time, they both overhear the voices of Madame Odintsova and Bazarov. These two are discussing whether or not Arkady has an attachment to Madame Odintsova. Bazarov is still certain that he is right, but Madame Odintsova doubts it. She is pleased with the brotherly manner of Arkady toward Katya. At this time, the couple pass out of the hearing range of Arkady and Katya.

After overhearing this embarrassing conversation, Arkady immediately confesses his love for Katya and discovers to his astonishment that she also loves him. The couple are then united "innocently weeping and laughing."

The next morning, Madame Odintsova shows Bazarov a letter from Arkady asking for Katya's hand in marriage.

Bazarov lends his support to the marriage, but announces his intention to rejoice at a distance. He plans to leave that day and return to his father's house. Madame Odintsova bids him goodbye, convinced that they shall meet again.

Bazarov congratulates Arkady and explains that marriage is good for certain types. He feels that Arkady was not meant to live the rough and difficult life demanded by "nihilism." Bazarov refuses to say anything sentimental in parting and only wishes his friend good luck. They embrace and part.

That evening in the presence of Katya, Arkady soon forgot his old companion. Madame Odintsova took great delight in observing the happy lovers, who were spending all their time together and avoiding everyone else's company.

Commentary

Even after Bazarov's arrival, Arkady still chooses to spend most of his time in the presence of Katya. In their talks, Arkady finally admits how much he has changed and how much Katya has been instrumental in his transition. Thus, from the beginning of the novel, we have observed the change that has taken place in Arkady until now he has become a responsible member of society desiring a wife and family.

As Arkady tries to propose to Katya, Bazarov, and Madame Odintsova pass close by, talking about the young couple. This is another example of Turgenev resorting to an artificial technique in order to develop his story. As in an earlier chapter, this technique carries little that is convincing in the realistic sense and strikes the reader as being false. But the overheard conversation does serve to prompt Arkady to make his proposal openly and directly.

The next day, when Bazarov hears about the marriage, he announces at the same time that he is leaving. It is almost too much for him to bear, since he has been so disappointed in his own efforts to earn the love of a woman. As he leaves, Madame Odintsova tells him that she is convinced they will meet again. The irony involved of course is the fact that they *will* have but one more meeting—at Bazarov's deathbed.

Bazarov does analyze Arkady's character correctly as he is leaving. He tells his friend: "you haven't either the audacity or malevolence...you were not created for our bitter, caustic, solitary life." In their final embrace, there seems to be a recognition that they have traveled along some good paths together and that they will never see each other again. There is finally no bitterness or regret, just a parting.

After Bazarov leaves, Madame Odintsova reiterates her earlier position that her peace is better than getting involved in his type of life. No one else missed Bazarov or noted his absence, especially Katya and Arkady, who by this time were oblivious to everything but each other.

CHAPTER 27

Summary

The old Bazarovs are extremely pleased to have their son home again. They promise to keep out of his way as he works. After a few days of hard work, Bazarov grew tired of his routine and became bored. His father thinks that he is embittered, but doesn't know what to do for him. Finally, he finds release in helping his father practice medicine, much to the delight of old Bazarov.

Later, Bazarov helps in an autopsy on a person who had died of typhoid and during the operation, he cut his finger. The doctor whom he was assisting had no antiseptic, thus Bazarov feels that he will probably contract the disease in a few days. His father is distressed beyond comprehension when he hears the news.

Three days later, Bazarov comes down with fever and must be tended by his father. Old Bazarov continues to tell himself that it is only a slight chill which will pass, but Bazarov tells him directly that he has typhoid fever. He is brutally frank with his father and tells him that he hadn't really expected to die so soon. Bazarov wants a message sent to Madame Odintsova telling her that he is dying. The old man promises to do so immediately.

Another doctor arrives and suggests that perhaps the fever will pass and that the patient will recover. Bazarov is not deluded and reminds the doctor that no patient has ever recovered from this condition.

Bazarov steadily grew worse, even though for a few hours at a time he would appear to be better. At one point, Old Bazarov asks his son to allow a priest to come to him, but Bazarov refuses for the present time.

Madame Odintsova arrives bringing with her a German doctor. Vassily Ivanovitch feels that she is a benefactress and that the German doctor will be able to save his son. While they are consulting, Odintsova goes in to see Bazarov. He is most appreciative that she came. He tells her how beautiful she is but warns her not to come too close to him. He talks to her more about their relationship and wants her to forget him as soon as he is dead. The next day he is dead.

Commentary

Bazarov is back with his parents, but he is possessed by the gloom and melancholy of a lovelorn romantic. We see that he tries to work but boredom and anxiety overtake him. His father also notices the peculiar behavior of his son. We can assume that his encounter with Madame Odintsova has affected the nihilist more than he is willing to admit.

Bazarov, himself a doctor, takes unnecessary chances in performing the autopsy as though he simply did not care whether he caught the disease or not. When he does know that he has the disease, he merely offers the sardonic comment that it really is unpleasant to die so soon. Then he assumes an extremely romantic role: he sends a note off to Madame Odintsova that he is dying. We then see the nihilist faced with death. In life he could negate everything, but no man is able to negate death, so Bazarov must now face this unpleasant fact.

As long as Bazarov is conscious he refuses the ministrations of the church and thus remains true to his beliefs in this respect. But he does comfort his father by reminding him that the last rites can be administered to an unconscious man.

During the death scene, Bazarov gives in to romantic inclinations when he talks with Madame Odintsova. He tells her how beautiful she is — a compliment that Bazarov would have earlier called a lot of romantic twaddle. As he becomes delirious, he says things which contradict his earlier views. He even recognizes that certain *types* of men are needed by Russia, and he, Bazarov, is not one of them.

CHAPTER 28

Summary

Six months later, Nikolai is giving a farewell dinner for Pavel. During the preceding week, Arkady married Katya and Nikolai married Fenichka. At the party, "Everyone served everyone else with comical attentiveness as if they had agreed to act out some kind of naive comedy." Pavel thanks everyone, embraces his brother, and bids them all farewell in English. Katya suggests to Arkady that they offer a secret toast in memory of Bazarov.

Turgenev briefly informs the reader what each of the characters has done with his life. Odintsova enters into a marriage of convenience with a lawyer and lives in great harmony and "perhaps love" with him. At Marino, the affairs are straightened out as Arkady takes over the farm and Nikolai tends to settling the arguments between the liberated serfs.

Pavel establishes himself in the highest circles of society in Dresden where he is know as "der Herr Baron von Kirsanov." Sitnikov roams around St. Petersburg and claims to be continuing the "work" of Bazarov. In a remote corner of Russia, there is a cemetery where one can sometimes observe two old people visiting the grave where young Bazarov is buried.

Commentary

There is very little to be said about the last chapter, since Turgenev says it all. That is, Turgenev uses the traditional nineteenth-century technique of rounding out the history of all of his characters.

The final chapter does make it clear that Arkady's transition is complete and he becomes the practical man of business who still adheres to many of the more advanced ideas but will not reject all the classical values found in art and literature and music. His father, then, is freed to arbitrate in disputes arising among the peasants and hired help.

Thus, the novel ends with a sense of all things having come to the right end and with everything in the proper perspective.

CHARACTER ANALYSES

Yevgeny Vassilievitch Bazarov

Bazarov is most often considered the central figure in the novel. He inculcates the central idea of "nihilism" and acts as the representative force of the new generation against which the older characters of traditional beliefs can react.

Bazarov is a nihilist of humble background whose life-view involves a rejection of anything that has previously been accepted as valid. The "nihilist" refuses to take anyone's word for anything; he can have no alliances and no emotions; he cares no more for one country than for another and accepts only that which is scientifically proven.

The purpose of the nihilist is to destroy all the existing institutions and values. He considers himself and his kind as a type of pure force whose purpose it is "to clear the site" of traditional values without any consideration of rebuilding or of replacing them with new ones. The ultimate end of the nihilist would seem to be self-destruction, because he can never let stand that which someone else has built and when all is destroyed, he must then turn inward.

When we first meet Bazarov, he adheres strictly to his philosophy of nihilism. In brief arguments with Pavel and others, he spurns art, literature, music, and even loyalty to one's country because none of these things have any meaning to him. As for love and romance, he feels that Pavel or any man who allows himself to be influenced by a woman is idiotic. He believes that if a woman appeals to you that you should have your way with her or leave her.

The first person who ever challenged Bazarov's views was Madame Odintsova. She believed in a type of "order" in her life, whereas the concept of "order" is in direct violation to the nihilist's way of thinking. Bazarov begins to sway in the presence of this grand lady. He knew very soon that he would never have his way with her and at the same time, he did not have the strength to leave her. He finds himself in a situation similar to the one he ridiculed Pavel for being in. Thus, a man who had previously ridiculed emotion and love, makes an empassioned declaration of love and after he realizes that he has made a fool of himself, he cannot return to his past security within the limits of his nihilistic philosophy.

Bazarov never abandons his earlier views, but they do become somewhat modified toward the end of the novel. His response to Fenichka and to his own parents indicates a slight change in his character. Furthermore, when he is dying, his romantic last desire to see Madame Odintsova suggests the degree to which he has strayed away from the concepts of pure "nihilism."

Arkady Nikolayevitch Kirsanov

Arkady undergoes the greatest development during the course of the novel. At first an immature young man, obsequiously following his friend Bazarov and the ideas fostered by him, Arkady eventually finds the strength to assert himself intellectually and emotionally.

He has a strong trace of his father's romanticism in his nature, but until he musters the strength to break from Bazarov and "nihilism" he keeps this side of himself in severe check. As Katya—his beloved and future wife—points out, he is not a nihilistic bird of prey, but rather a domesticated, good-natured creature.

Arkady's relationship with people seems a great deal more wholesome than Bazarov's—he loves and admires certain aspects of his father, he fulfills himself with Katya, and understands his uncle Pavel well enough to offer a good defense of Pavel's character.

Arkady has always been acting somewhat against his nature by following the concept of the nihilist. Basically, he enjoys good music, especially as played by Katya, good art, and the value of tradition. But he also likes to be as modern and as liberal as possible. Thus, one can easily see in this character a positive force in the novel which combines some of the valuable "practical" ideas of the new generation without stripping life to a barren wasteland by abolishing all forms of art, belief, and love. In the final scenes, we see that Arkady was able to make a success out of the deteriorating farm and became a contented married man conducting his farm in keeping with the latest progressive ideas.

Anna Sergeyevna Odintsova

Madame Odintsova is twenty-nine years old, but during her short life she has experienced much and seen a great deal of the world. She had earlier married a very rich man who was considerably older than she. She accepted him because of his age and his ordered way of life. When he died and left her a rich lady, she traveled through various parts of Europe before deciding to return to the provinces to settle down.

Madame Odintsova is not liked in the province because she is a woman with too many liberal ideas. When she meets Arkady, she asks about Bazarov because she wants to know a person who has had the courage "not to believe in anything." This desire to meet Bazarov is a result of Madame Odintsova's cold and austere personality. She has decided to remove herself from all the anxieties of life, and in meeting Bazarov, she hopes to see what someone else's different and unique response is to the problem of living.

For Madame Odintsova, the ultimate concern is to maintain peace and order. She runs her household and estate in a precise orderly fashion, and virtually never strays from the bounds she has imposed upon life. She believes that "without order, life would be too boring." Her reluctance to become attached to Bazarov is actually based upon the fear of being taken away from her ordered existence and led into unknown seas. For her, "peace is after all the best thing in life." Thus, she remains cold and austere even to the end.

Pavel Petrovitch Kirsanov

Pavel is a "dated" aristocratic gentleman who belongs to a rapidly fleeting era in Russian history. He is caught in the dilemma of having to witness the facts of social change without being able to accept them either emotionally or intellectually. Needless to say his reaction to Bazarov and the new "nihilism" is fierce.

Pavel is the true fop, meticulous about his dress and general deportment, but totally hollow in his adherence to the ideals of the aristocracy, and ineffective in all of his actions. For all of his gentility and correctness, he serves no useful function in this life. The only advice he can offer Nikolai when the latter's estate is falling into ruin is *"Du calme! Du calme!"* But our judgment of Pavel is not really too harsh. At times we cannot help pitying this man who has experienced a tragically sad love affair and who sees his way of life crumbling about him. Also, he does exhibit something of a magnanimous spirit when he finally condones, if he doesn't actually approve, the marriage between his brother Nikolai and the servant girl Fenichka. By the end of the novel he has not changed in the least, however, and we leave him playing the role of an aristocratic, bored nobleman in Dresden.

Nikolai Petrovitch Kirsanov

Nikolai is the romantic father of Arkady, who has tried his best to keep up with modern ideas in an effort to remain close to his son. But when Arkady returns home bringing with him a nihilist with whom he apparently agrees, Nikolai feels that there is a great gulf now between the two generations.

Nikolai has very little of the practical in his nature. It is very difficult for him to tend to the business of running the farm. To keep abreast of the most recent ideas, he has freed all of his serfs and is trying to run the estate on a rental basis, but he cannot make it work. Slowly the farm is deteriorating.

While the farm sinks into neglect, Nikolai is often seen dreaming of his past life and remembering events of long ago. He also spends much time reading the romantic Pushkin and playing music on the cello. His greatness lies in his generous and expansive nature and his appreciation for beauty, but his flaw is that he lives too much in an impractical dream world. Unlike Pavel, he does not judge the younger generation too harshly, and by his patient waiting, is finally rewarded by being reunited with his son.

STRUCTURE OF *FATHERS AND SONS*

In many of Turgenev's novels, it is difficult to detect a discernible structure. His greatness often lies with the individual scenes rather than with the total work. The Russian literary critic Avrahm

Yarmolinsky says that "the total effect of *Fathers and Sons* does not measure up to that of individual scenes, so that the whole is less than the sum of its parts." This critic does not mean to imply that Turgenev had no structure, but that the greatness of the novel is best found by the manner in which individual scenes are rendered so powerfully.

The overall structure of the novel is seen through the journeys which the young students make. Furthermore, if we keep the title constantly in mind, we see that the author is building these journeys around the fulcrum of each of the two sons in relationship with his father. Thus there is a type of structure which involves Arkady and Bazarov meeting Arkady's father, and then leaving to meet Bazarov's father. This allows the reader to perceive large and sweeping contrasts.

The purpose of the journeys also influences the development of the structure. We have two types of students or young men. We want to see their basic philosophy of nihilism in action in many types of situations. Thus the novel opens by showing how nihilism evokes certain responses in the older landowning family of the Kirsanovs. Furthermore, here Bazarov comes into conflict with a representative of the old school of romanticism. In the opening portions of the novel, we observe drastic conflicts of opinions. Following this, Turgenev must move to another scene in which we can observe the same nihilistic theories in practice in another environment.

The confrontation with the second set of parents must be withheld until we see Bazarov and Arkady on some neutral ground. This leads them to the house of the liberal and intelligent Madame Odintsova. Here we see that Bazarov is not as adamant in his philosophy as he was in the presence of the romantic Nikolai or the effete Pavel Kirsanov.

The novel eventually moves to a confrontation with Bazarov's parents. During the scenes in the Bazarov house, we note a striking difference between the two young people. Thus, Turgenev has chosen a structure which allows his characters to reveal certain aspects of their personality and their philosophical views dramatically by bringing them into contact with many different aspects of life. After the visit to the Bazarov house, note how Turgenev symbolically presents the rift between Arkady and Bazarov by having each one go off on a separate voyage of his own.

In general, Turgenev has utilized a structure of movement back and forth in order to develop his theme of the new and radical in confrontation with the old and the traditional. To embody this theme, it is necessary for the main characters to move from one place to another in order to come into contact with various ideas in juxtaposition with which their own ideas are tested and evaluated.

REVIEW QUESTIONS

1. Consider briefly what each of the central characters' definition of the term "nihilism" would be.

2. What seems to be Turgenev's judgment of the philosophic concepts of "nihilism"?

3. What alternatives does Turgenev offer to the new generation's philosophy?

4. How do such general motifs as the idea of the *bildungsroman* (the development of a young man) and the traditional conflicts between successive generations function in the novel?

5. How does Turgenev make use of humor to present his themes in the novel? For example, satire, parody, humorous and dramatic situations. Does his use of humor enhance the story?

6. What kind of judgment can we assume Tugenev is making about Nikolai's romanticism and Romanticism in general?

7. What assumption can be made about Arkady's and Bazarov's characters by observing the manner in which they treat their own parents and each other's parents?

8. How does Madame Odintsova contradict Bazarov's nihilistic views?

9. How does Fenichka function in the novel? How would the novel be different if she were omitted?

10. What is the function of Sitnikov and Kukshina? How effective is Turgenev's presentation of these characters?

11. What is the difference between Piotr and Prokofitch as servants?

12. What are the central events which bring about Arkady's change?

SELECTED BIBLIOGRAPHY

Freeborn, Richard. *Turgenev: The Novelist's Novelist*. New York: Oxford University Press, 1960.

Gettmann, Royal A. *Turgenev in England and America.* "Illinois Studies in Language and Literature," V, 27, No. 2. Urbana, 1941.

Granjard, Henri. *Ivan Tourguenev et les courants politiques et sociaux de son Temps*. Paris, 1953.

Wilson, Edmund. "Preface" to *Literary Reminiscences and Autobiographical Fragments*. New York: Vintage Press, 1958.

Yarmolinsky, Avrahm. *Turgenev: The Man, His Art and His Age*. New York: The Orion Press, 1959.

– – –. "Turgenev: A Reevaluation," Introduction to the *Vintage Turgenev*. New York: Vintage Books, 1960.

NOTES

NOTES

NOTES

NOTES

NOTES

NOTES